HOW *Government* WORKS

Vetoing Bills

Derek Miller

Cavendish Square
New York

Published in 2019 by Cavendish Square Publishing, LLC
243 5th Avenue, Suite 136, New York, NY 10016

First Edition

Library of Congress Cataloging-in-Publication Data

Names: Miller, Derek L., author.
Title: Vetoing bills / Derek Miller.
Description: First edition. | New York, NY : Cavendish Square, 2019. |
Series: How government works | Audience: 5-8. | Includes bibliographical references and index.
Identifiers: LCCN 2018026121 (print) | LCCN 2018034683 (ebook) |
ISBN 9781502641601 (ebook) | ISBN 9781502641595 (library bound) | ISBN 9781502641588 (pbk.)
Subjects: LCSH: Veto--United States--Juvenile literature. |
Legislative veto--United States--Juvenile literature. | Item veto--United States--Juvenile literature. |
United States--Politics and government--Juvenile literature.
Classification: LCC JK586 (ebook) | LCC JK586 .M56 2019 (print) | DDC 352.23/5--dc23
LC record available at https://lccn.loc.gov/2018026121

Editorial Director: David McNamara
Editor: Caitlyn Miller
Copy Editor: Alex Tessman
Associate Art Director: Alan Sliwinski
Designer: Christina Shults
Production Coordinator: Karol Szymczuk
Photo Research: J8 Media

The photographs in this book are used by permission and through the courtesy of:
Cover Brendan Smialowski/AFP/Getty Images; p. 4 Alexander Shcherbak/TASS/Getty Images; p. 7 Orhan Cam/Shutterstock.com; pp. 8, 9, 12 Pool/Getty Images; p. 14 Mark Wilson/Getty Images; p. 17 Jim Watson/AFP/Getty Images; p. 18 Cg-realms/modified by Philosopher/Wikimedia Commons/ File:2010 census reapportionment.svg/CC0; p. 23 DEA Picture Library/De Agostini/ Getty Images; p. 24 Bettmann/Getty Images; p. 29 Wally McNamee/Corbis Historical/Getty Images; p. 30 Everett Historical/Shutterstock.com; p. 34 Don Carl Steffen/ Gamma-Rapho/ Getty Images; p. 39 Robert J Fisch/Moment/Getty Images; p. 40 Barry Iverson/The LIFE Images Collection/Getty Images; p. 42 Gabriel Bouys/AFP/Getty Images; p. 44 Encyclopaedia Britannica/Universal Images Group/Getty Images; p. 46 Drop of Light/Shutterstock.com; p. 49 The White House/Getty Images; p. 53 Gary Cameron/REUTERS/Newscom; p. 55 The Washington Post/Getty Images; design elements throughout Supermimicry/Shutterstock.com.

Printed in the United States of America

CONTENTS

1 *What Is a Veto?*

The American government is run according to laws. Congresspeople are responsible for writing laws. With enough support, the bills that Congress writes become laws. But the president has the power to veto a bill that Congress passes. This sends the bill back to Congress. Once a vetoed bill is sent back to Congress, they can make major changes to it, override the veto, or abandon the bill. It is possible for Congress to override a veto with enough votes, but this is rare. Presidents wield a great deal

Opposite: Like all presidents, President Donald Trump has the power to veto bills.

of power from their ability to veto bills. They can shape the laws of the country using their veto power.

The American Government

According to the US Constitution, power stems from the people. The people vote for politicians to represent them in Washington, DC, and state capitals. These politicians are responsible for passing new laws. Laws govern what people cannot do, like laws against stealing, but laws also say what the government does do. Laws are responsible for the government's ability to maintain and build roads, pay for schools, and distribute money to retirees.

Before looking at how bills are passed and how the president can veto them, we need to look at the structure of the government. The federal government is the government based out of Washington, DC. It governs the entire country. It wields more power than individual state or local governments, which have a limited area of power.

The Constitution divides the federal government into three different branches: the legislative, executive, and judicial branches. This division is an important part of understanding how the government works. Each branch is ultimately responsible to the American people.

The legislative branch is Congress. Congress is made up of the Senate and the House of Representatives. Members of both chambers are elected directly by the people of individual states. Their job is to legislate—or write laws. "Legislation" is another word for "law." For

Congress meets in the US Capitol Building in Washington, DC.

a law to pass, it requires both chambers of Congress to approve it.

The executive branch is headed by the president. Every four years, the president is elected by people around the country. It is the president's job to enforce the laws that Congress passes. Additionally, the president is the head of the armed forces and the country's chief representative to foreign governments. The power to veto bills that he or she disagrees with is another way for the president to wield power.

The judicial branch is composed of federal judges. These judges are appointed by the president and approved by the Senate. While not directly picked by the American people, they are chosen by people elected by the people.

Members of the Supreme Court, the highest court in the land, gather to hear a presidential address.

Judges hear court cases and decide on controversial issues. If there is some question of how a law should be put into action, it may go before a judge. They also hear cases of wrongdoing. Judges have no role in passing legislation. However, they do have some limited but important power once a new law goes into effect. If someone challenges the law, judges can rule it unconstitutional, or, in effect, illegal.

How a Bill Becomes Law

The legislative process is a key part of the American government. The passage of new laws is how the government changes over time. At its heart, passing new laws is the responsibility of the legislative branch. But the ability to veto bills gives the president important influence over the process.

All bills begin in Congress. They can begin in either the Senate or the House of Representatives. Any senator or representative can introduce a bill. Often, bills will have cosponsors—other congresspeople who support the measure. Once a bill is introduced, it is assigned to a committee. There are committees in both the House and the Senate. Committees are composed of a small number of representatives or senators.

Committees are the expert bodies that first consider a bill and give their opinion on the issue. Sometimes, large bills are even split into different parts that are sent to different committees. There are about twenty committees in each chamber—the exact number changes over time. Committees specialize in different areas. For example, both the House and Senate have agriculture, budget, and veteran's affairs committees. Bills that affect these areas would go to those committees first. If a large bill affected both veteran's affairs and the budget, it might be divided into parts to be sent to both committees.

President Trump and congressional leaders from both political parties work together to discuss legislation in 2017.

The committee debates the bill. They often call in experts in a field to give their opinion. The committee has the power to modify

George Washington and the Veto

The first president of the United States was George Washington. He served two terms, from 1789 to 1797. In these eight years, he vetoed just two bills. On April 5, 1792, Washington exercised the first presidential veto in American history. Strangely, he vetoed a bill not because he disagreed with it but because he argued it was unconstitutional. The bill was to apportion (assign a number of) representatives to the states. The number of representatives each state has depends on the state's population, and it is a matter that Congress must decide. The Constitution says that there can be no more than one representative per thirty thousand people. The bill Washington vetoed broke this rule. As a result, Congress created a new system of apportioning representatives that followed rules in the Constitution.

In 1797, Washington vetoed his second bill. This veto was more typical. He disagreed with a measure taken by Congress to change the structure of the military. As a result, he returned the bill, along with a list of his objections, to Congress. Neither of Washington's vetoes were overridden by Congress. However, by modern standards he issued very few vetoes. Early presidents tended to veto few, if any, bills. Most presidents in recent years have vetoed at least ten. Three presidents of the twentieth century vetoed hundreds.

the bill at this stage. If they think there is some problem or improvement to be made, they can change the bill before voting on it. If a majority of a committee vote in favor of a bill, it is returned to the House or the Senate for debate. (If a majority do not vote for it, the bill does not move forward, and it does not become law.)

If the bill does move forward, it is once again debated. This time, all the members of the House or Senate can express their opinion—not just committee members. The full chamber votes on the bill. If a majority vote for the measure, the bill is sent to the other chamber of Congress. For instance, if a bill begins in the Senate and the Senate votes to pass it, the bill then goes to the House. The process largely starts over again in the other chamber. The other committee considers the bill and votes on it. If the bill passes this vote, it goes before the entire chamber, where it must once again gain a majority of votes.

Sometimes, a slightly different bill is passed by the House and the Senate. The two versions then go before a conference committee. This committee works to create an acceptable version for both chambers. Once they reach an agreement, both chambers need to vote on the bill again.

If both chambers vote to pass a bill, it then goes to the president. At this point, the president can do one of three things. The president can sign the bill. This completes the legislative process and makes it a law. The president can do nothing. After ten days, the bill then becomes law.

President Trump signs a bill to make it a law, rather than vetoing it.

However, the president did not need to attach his or her name to the new law. The third option is the presidential veto. Vetoing a bill signals the president's disapproval of the bill. It returns the bill to Congress.

Congress has the power to override the presidential veto, but only if two-thirds of both chambers vote in favor of the bill. In practice, this level of support and willingness to oppose the wishes of the president is rare. Less than 5 percent of presidential vetoes have been overridden by Congress. If the veto is overridden, the bill becomes law without the signature of the president.

Vetoing and the Constitution

The president's power to veto bills is written into the Constitution. Vetoing a bill is a key part of how the branches of government interact. It allows the president to limit the power of Congress. Article 1, Section 7, of the Constitution spells out how a veto works:

> *Every Bill which shall have passed the House of Representatives and the Senate, shall, before it become a Law, be presented to the President of the United States; If he approve he shall sign it, but if not he shall return it, with his Objections to that House in which it shall have originated … If after such Reconsideration two thirds of that House shall agree to pass the Bill, it shall be sent, together with the Objections, to the other House, by which it shall likewise be reconsidered, and if approved by two thirds of that House, it shall become a Law.*

While the power to veto is outlined in the Constitution, the specifics of presidential vetoes are sometimes controversial. Presidents have interpreted the Constitution differently when it comes to how far their power reaches. At times, the three branches of government have come into conflict on how exactly vetoes function. We will examine these cases throughout the next chapter and see just how far presidential power reaches.

2 *Who Vetoes Bills?*

The president is the only person in the federal government who can veto bills. While the president may ask advice from their advisors on the issue, the decision is the president's alone. At the state level, governors can also veto bills. Each state has its own constitution that outlines the structure of the state government. But in all fifty states, that constitution gives the governor the power to veto legislation.

Opposite: Former presidents Barack Obama (*left*) and George W. Bush (*center*) vetoed twelve bills each, while Bill Clinton (*right*) vetoed thirty-seven.

Checks and Balances

The American government is a finely tuned system. Its three branches all have various checks and balances to limit the other branches' power. The three branches have different roles to play in the government, but they are able to interact to a limited degree. This interaction prevents one branch from gaining too much power.

The power to veto a bill is one of the most important checks on power that exists in the Constitution. It allows the president to greatly increase the number of votes needed by Congress to pass legislation. Without the veto, if one political party controlled a narrow majority of the House and Senate, that party could pass law after law. With the veto, Congress and the president must be united, or Congress must have a two-thirds majority.

There are many other checks and balances in American government. One of the most important is the ability of judges to declare a law unconstitutional. For instance, if Congress passed a law forbidding the president from vetoing bills, the courts would overturn it. The power for the presidential veto is taken directly from the Constitution. Congress cannot get rid of it. In the same way, when the president refuses to enforce laws that Congress passes, courts rule that refusal unconstitutional. It is the president's role to uphold the laws of the land. The president can veto them before they are passed, but once passed, they must be upheld.

Other checks and balances structure many interactions between the branches of government. For example, the

President Donald Trump and his cabinet meet in the White House on January 10, 2018.

president gets to pick his or her cabinet—the heads of the departments of the federal government and the president's closest advisors. However, the Senate must approve the president's choices. Likewise, the president appoints federal judges—but only with the approval of the Senate. In extraordinary cases, Congress also has the power to remove the president from office, but this has never occurred.

Consensus Building and Compromise

This system of checks and balances means that the American government is relatively slow moving. This was the intent of the writers of the Constitution. They

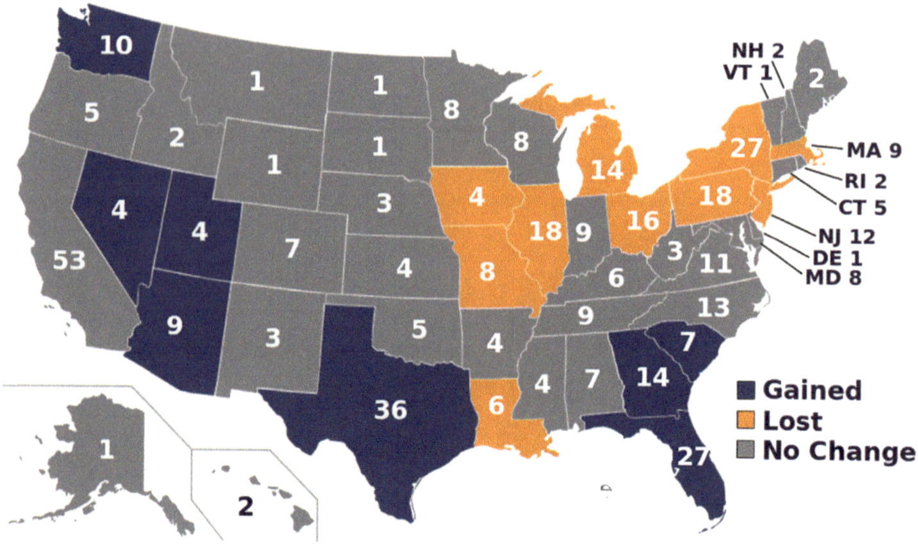

This map shows the total number of representatives that each state has in the House, as of 2018. States in yellow saw their number decrease since 2010 while states in blue saw their number increase.

did not want every election to signal a massive shift in American policy. They imagined a government that would adapt slowly over time. Large changes are easiest to accomplish when they enjoy wide popular support.

One significant way this is written into the Constitution is the bicameral legislature. A legislature is bicameral when it is made up of two chambers. The very existence of two chambers slows the process of law-making to some degree. Bills need to be supported by a majority of lawmakers in both chambers. Additionally, the Senate is composed of two senators from each state—regardless of the state's population. In the House, states are represented according to their population. This means states with few people, like Alaska, Delaware, and Wyoming, have just one representative, while California has fifty-three!

This system prevents larger states from dominating the legislature. Even if a few large states want a change to the law, they cannot pass a law without support from senators who represent small and large states equally. The purpose of this, as well as the presidential veto, is to create a system that relies on compromise and consensus building. Compromise is when two opposing sides come together and meet in the middle. They may disagree on an issue, but they both give something up to reach an agreement both sides can live with. A consensus is when both sides can agree on something. They may have different opinions on other issues, but they can come together on at least one issue. Compromise and consensus are the bedrock of the American system of government.

The presidential veto is an important part of this system. Even the threat of a veto is often enough to make Congress pass a bill that is more acceptable to both parties. Alternatively, if Congress is trying to legislate on an issue with a narrow majority, the president can block it. This encourages Congress to try to gain more support for a measure.

Roles of the President

The president has a number of jobs according to the Constitution. While the veto is an important presidential power, it is not the focus of the presidency. Experts usually give the president the following six roles, although others are sometimes included as well.

Head of State

The head of state of a country is its leader. The president is the symbol of the American people. In some countries, this role is not held by a powerful political figure. For instance, in the United Kingdom, the Queen is the head of state, but she has little real power. In the United States, the title of head of state and the vast powers of the presidency are held by one individual.

Chief Executive

The president is the chief executive of the federal government. He or she must execute the laws of the land faithfully and oversee the government. In this role, the president is similar to the chief executive officer (CEO) of a massive company: the executive branch of the federal government has more than two million employees. The day-to-day functions of most of the government is overseen by the president's cabinet. The fact that cabinet members must be approved by the Senate is a significant check on the president's power.

Chief Diplomat

The president is the representative of the country abroad. He or she appoints ambassadors to other countries. The president shapes foreign policy—the way that the United

States interacts with other countries in friendship and in war. However, the Senate has many important checks on the president's power to do this. For instance, it must approve the appointment of ambassadors and vote on treaties with foreign countries.

Commander in Chief

The president is commander in chief of the armed forces and outranks every general and admiral. It is the duty of the president to oversee the Army, Navy, Air Force, Coast Guard, and Marine Corps. The president directs the armed forces during conflicts. This power is checked by the fact that only Congress can declare war. In practice, this check on the president's power has been weakened in recent years. Most modern armed conflicts have been waged without a formal declaration of war.

Chief Legislator

The president is the chief legislator. This is one role of the president that has limited power behind it. When campaigning for office, the president will put forward a legislative agenda—laws that he or she wants to see passed. However, it is ultimately up to Congress to write these laws and then vote on them. The only power the president has when it comes to legislating is the veto. While it is an important power for blocking legislation, the veto power does nothing to pass laws. The president relies on Congress to do this. The fact that the president won an election is often seen as support for their legislative agenda, but this does not guarantee congressional action.

Chief of Party

The Constitution does not mention political parties, but throughout American history there has been a two-party system. Today, those two political parties are the Democrats and Republicans. Every president has come from one of the two major parties of his day. Since the president won a general election, he is looked to as the leader of his party who determines what to do next.

The Evolution of the Veto

The use of the presidential veto has changed and evolved over American history. Most of the early presidents used it only to block unconstitutional laws. Whether or not it should be used to change government policy was a matter of some debate. For instance, Alexander Hamilton and Thomas Jefferson, two members of George Washington's cabinet, had very different ideas of how the veto should be used. Even the authors of the Constitution disagreed on its interpretation.

Alexander Hamilton argued that the veto was a tool that the president should use to block "improper laws." Improper laws were not necessarily unconstitutional, he thought. They could simply be poorly thought out or impractical. Meanwhile, Thomas Jefferson believed that only unconstitutional laws ought to be vetoed. He did not think it was the role of the president to

President Andrew Jackson was the first president to use the veto more than a handful of times.

stop Congress from legislating. The veto was simply a tool the president could use to protect his or her own executive power. If Congress tried to overstep its role, it should be checked with the veto, but the veto had no place in policy debates.

Early presidents differed on how exactly they saw the veto. As a whole, they were much more conservative on the issue than modern presidents. Of the first thirteen presidents, six never vetoed a single bill. In fact, Thomas Jefferson was the only two-term president to never veto a bill. However, his dislike of the veto as a policy tool was never truly put to the test. He enjoyed near total support from a Congress dominated by his party.

The first president to use the veto more freely was Andrew Jackson, the seventh president. He vetoed more bills than the previous six presidents before him combined. In 1832, Jackson vetoed the popular Bank Bill that continued the use of a central bank for the whole country. Not only was the bill supported by the majority of Congress and the public, the issue had already been ruled constitutional by the Supreme Court. It was a great expansion of the power of the veto as well as the

Franklin D. Roosevelt and the Veto

One president in American history broke the record for the most vetoes by a large margin. Franklin D. Roosevelt (FDR) vetoed an extraordinary 635 pieces of legislation. For comparison, Barack Obama and George W. Bush vetoed only twelve bills. Surprisingly,

Franklin D. Roosevelt in the Oval Office in 1945

FDR's party (the Democrats) had a significant majority in both the House and Senate throughout his twelve years in office. Nevertheless, FDR repeatedly vetoed various bills they passed. Only nine of his vetoes were overridden.

FDR is remembered as one of the most powerful presidents in history. He exercised executive power to a degree rarely seen before. He was the only president to be elected for more than two terms—a tradition that George Washington began. After his death during his fourth term, a constitutional amendment was passed limiting presidents to two terms as a result.

FDR's relationship with Congress was troubled, and this can be seen in his vetoes. He was the first president to personally read a veto message aloud to a joint session of Congress. Additionally, he was the first to veto a revenue act (an act to fund the government with money). FDR said the act was a "tax relief bill providing relief not for the needy but for the greedy." His veto was overridden by Congress.

presidency. The veto prompted Henry Clay—considered one of the most important senators in American history—to say, "The veto is an extraordinary power, which … was not expected, by the convention, to be used in ordinary cases." Like Jefferson, Clay thought the veto was not meant to block bills the president simply did not like. Most presidents have preferred Jackson's view of the veto's far-ranging power over Clay and Jefferson's view.

Grover Cleveland, who held office between 1885 to 1889 and then once again between 1893 and 1897, was the first president to veto hundreds of bills. Over the course of his two terms, he vetoed 574 bills. This was the most vetoes of any president per year in office. Cleveland, a Democrat, rigidly opposed the Republican Congress of the time. He vetoed bill after bill that would have resulted in more government spending, arguing that the role of the government should be small. His most famous veto was one that stopped relief to Texan farmers affected by a massive drought. In part, he wrote, "though the people support the Government, the Government should not support the people." It was a forceful argument for small government, but also an idea that has fallen out of favor.

Since Cleveland, only three other presidents have issued more than a hundred vetoes: Franklin D. Roosevelt and the two presidents that followed him, Harry S. Truman and Dwight D. Eisenhower. While the presidents of the twentieth century believed that they had the right to veto bills they simply disagreed with, few needed to exercise this power so frequently.

A Different Kind of Veto

The president has ten days to veto a bill Congress passes. If he or she does nothing, the bill becomes law. However, there is an important exception to this. It is written into the Constitution, which reads, "If any Bill shall not be returned by the President within ten Days (Sundays excepted) after it shall have been presented to him, the Same shall be a Law, in like Manner as if he had signed it, unless the Congress by their Adjournment prevent its Return, in which Case it shall not be a Law." In other words, if Congress adjourns—or stops meeting for the year—the president can simply not sign a bill, and it does not become a law. This makes sense since there is no Congress for the president to return the bill to, as is required by a normal veto.

This is called a "pocket veto" because the president "pockets" a bill and does nothing. When this occurs, it functions as a veto that cannot be overridden. This may seem like an extraordinary power for the president to have since Congress cannot override it. But the president cannot decide to pocket veto any bill he or she wishes. The bill must be delivered to the president within a ten-day period of Congress adjourning for the year.

Despite this restriction, pocket vetoes are surprisingly common. This is because Congress often passes a great number of laws just before adjourning. This practice makes the pocket veto a convenient tool that presidents have used a great deal. In theory, Congress could pass the same or a similar bill after the president pocket vetoes it. However, they rarely have the support to override a typical veto, so this is not common. More often, Congress works with the president to write a new bill that will not be vetoed, or they abandon the effort entirely.

While the Constitution seems quite clear on the pocket veto, it is subject to some controversy. Most of the argument centers on what exactly "Adjournment" means in the Constitution. Either chamber of Congress can adjourn for up to three days without consulting the other chamber. For longer adjournments, both chambers must agree. Some presidents have tried to pocket veto bills in these brief three-day adjournments. However, court decisions have decided this is unconstitutional. The House or Senate can appoint someone to receive messages from the president for short adjournments, allowing a veto and making a pocket veto unconstitutional.

One gray area that still exists is whether a president can pocket veto legislation between the two sessions of Congress. Each Congress is in office two years. Then, after elections, a different session of Congress begins. Typically, Congress has one session each year for a total of two sessions. However, there is an adjournment between

President Gerald R. Ford was the first president to use the controversial protective return pocket veto.

the two sessions. Many presidents have claimed to pocket veto a bill in this break between sessions. However, Congress often argues that is not possible. So far, it remains unclear if these are truly pocket vetoes. Courts have not ruled on the matter. As a result, Congress and the president sometimes come into conflict over whether a veto was a pocket veto, can be overridden, or should be interpreted as law (since the president failed to sign it in ten days).

As a result of this uncertainty, some president have used the protective return pocket veto. They claim to pocket veto a bill, while also sending a message to Congress that they are vetoing it. Pocket vetoes do not include messages. By their definition, they occur when the president does not return the bill with a message to Congress. Congress and many scholars argue that the protective return veto is unconstitutional. The president may pocket veto or return a bill with a statement. However, the president does not have the power to veto and pocket veto the same bill.

President Gerald R. Ford was the first president to use a protective return pocket veto. Congress overrode one of his attempts—rejecting the idea it was a pocket veto. Since Ford gave in and did not challenge this in court, the constitutionality of a protective return pocket veto is undecided. A number of presidents since Ford have issued them, including Barack Obama and George W. Bush.

President James Monroe issued the first signing statement.

Vetoing Part of a Bill

The Constitution does not allow the president to veto part of a bill. The president must either allow the bill to become law or veto it in its entirety. However, presidents throughout history have tried a number of strategies to effectively veto just part of a bill.

One measure some presidents have used is a signing statement. This is an official statement the president issues as a bill is signed into law. Signing statements can take many forms. The first one was issued by James Monroe in 1822. He issued a statement saying that the new law was unclear in his opinion, and he spelled out how he would interpret the law when he enforced it. In 1842, John Tyler issued a different kind of signing statement. He wanted to state that a law was, in his opinion, unconstitutional. However, he was not so certain that he would veto it or refuse to enforce it.

Under George W. Bush, the presidency began issuing signing statements that argued parts of laws were unconstitutional, and they would not be enforced. This was an extremely controversial move. The American Bar Association (a professional association of lawyers) assembled a task force of experts to study the issue. They found that signing statements like those Bush issued "undermine the rule of law and our constitutional system of separation of powers." Bush stopped issuing so many after the report was published. However, when Barack Obama became president, he continued the tradition.

The legality of signing statements is a difficult issue. Because they are simply statements, they cannot be unconstitutional. If the president acts in line with a critical signing statement and refuses to enforce legislation, then the president can be taken to court. Opponents of signing statements argue that the president must simply veto a bill if part of it is unconstitutional. Then, if the veto is overridden, it is up to the courts to decide if the law is constitutional.

The second tool that was used to veto a part of a bill was the line-item veto. The line-item veto allowed the president to veto individual lines of appropriations bills. Appropriations bills fund the federal government. They distribute money to the various departments and agencies.

The line-item veto allowed the president to cut spending by vetoing certain lines of these bills.

The line-item veto was a power granted to the president by a law. In a rather strange turn of events, a Republican-controlled Congress passed the Line Item Veto Act of 1996 to give this power to Democratic president Bill Clinton. Republicans were concerned about deficit spending. Deficit spending is when the government spends more money than it raises through taxes. It results in government debt since the money must be borrowed. Bill Clinton signed the Line Item Veto Act into law even though many Democrats were opposed to it.

The line-item veto was short-lived. Just two years after the bill was signed into law, the Supreme Court ruled that the Line Item Veto Act was unconstitutional. There is nothing in the Constitution that says the president can veto part of a bill. The president could veto the entire bill or allow it to become law. The court ruled there was no middle ground. It also ruled Congress could not give the president such a sweeping new power.

Signing statements are sometimes compared to line-item vetoes. However, they are used with bills other than appropriations bills. Critics say that presidents sometimes use signing statements as a line-item veto. They allow them to sign a bill into law and then refuse to enforce part of it. Since line-item vetoes are unconstitutional, critics say that signing statements should be as well.

Clinton v. City of New York

When Congress passed the Line Item Veto Act of 1996, it was immediately challenged in court. Six members of Congress brought a case against the president, arguing that the new law was unconstitutional: the president had the power to veto bills in their entirety, or not at all. They argued the president could not pick and choose what sections of a budget bill to veto and sign the rest into law. This first court case was thrown out. Judges ruled that the congresspeople lacked standing—or a personal connection to the issue. Standing is required to bring a lawsuit against another party. While the congresspeople were lawmakers, this was not enough to give them standing. They had never suffered personal harm from a line-item veto.

In 1998, the Supreme Court did hear a case regarding the law. This time the court found that the city of New York did have standing. President Clinton had line-item vetoed a part of a bill that would have given $2.6 billion to the state of New York. The Supreme Court decided that the Line Item Veto Act was unconstitutional. Six of the justices agreed with this decision, while only three objected. The reasoning of the court was straightforward. A bill must be vetoed in its entirety—and not become law—or it must all become law. The fact that the Constitution did not allow a president a partial veto was the same as forbidding it. Congress could not give the president a new constitutional power.

3 *Vetoes in Action*

From George Washington's first veto to the end of Barack Obama's term as president in 2017, presidents exercised their power to veto a total of 2,574 times. Many of these vetoes were of minor bills that did not greatly impact history. But some vetoes are highly controversial. We will look at three of the most significant and controversial vetoes of recent years.

Universal Childcare

Families in which both parents work face the problem of how to look after their

Opposite: Universal child care would likely be available in the United States were it not for President Richard Nixon's veto.

children who are too young to go to school during the day. This is a relatively recent issue that entered the national spotlight in the 1970s. Early in American history, relatively few women worked, so they were able to watch children during the day. For instance, in 1920, just 20 percent of employed people were women. But greater equal rights for women during the 1960s made it possible for them to enter the workforce in larger numbers.

By 1971, nearly one in three mothers with a preschool-age child was working outside the home. Childcare was a serious problem for many families. While daycares were available, they were quite expensive. To tackle this issue, Congress drafted the Comprehensive Child Development Act. It created a national system of local childcare centers to mind children and provide them with medical care and early education.

The bill enjoyed bipartisan support, or support from both political parties. In the end, it passed in the Senate with 63 votes for it and 17 against it. In the House, it won by a much narrower margin of 210 to 186. It would have been a piece of landmark legislation, expanding the role of the government into the lives of young children across the country. People in favor argued that it was necessary for working families across the country to have access to affordable childcare. This in turn allowed them to work and contribute to the economy. Opponents argued it was a vast expansion of the government that should not happen. They also claimed it weakened the family as the basis of society.

President Nixon (the president at the time) asked his aides to draw up two statements: one if he signed the bill into law and a veto message if he rejected it. In the end, Nixon decided to veto it. He said he did so for three reasons. First, it was expensive. Second, the bill was unclear about how the childcare system would look. Third, he felt it weakened the family. Nixon's veto message was especially concerned with this third point. The author of the message, Pat Buchanan, was a strong defender of the traditional family. He wrote that the bill would "commit the vast moral authority of the National Government to the side of communal approaches to child rearing over against the family-centered approach."

Congress failed to override Nixon's veto, or pass a much less expensive and far-reaching bill that was drafted afterward. As a result, the United States still does not have a government-sponsored childcare program that covers all young children. Childcare costs like daycare are one of the largest expenses for American families. The government does very little to help families with these costs. Of the thirty-five countries that make up the Organization for Economic Development and Cooperation (OECD), the United States is third from the bottom in public spending on family benefits. This is due to in large part to Nixon's veto.

The War in Iraq

On September 11, 2001, the United States suffered the worst terror attack on its soil in history. Terrorists hijacked four commercial flights and flew the planes into the Twin

The First Override of a Veto

In April of 1841, President William Henry Harrison died just one month after being sworn into the office. His vice president, John Tyler, took the oath of office and replaced him. It was the first time in American history that a president had died and power changed hands without an election.

John Tyler, like Harrison and Congress at the time, belonged to the Whig political party. He was chosen to be vice president because he was a Southerner. Harrison was from the North, and it was hoped that Tyler would win votes from Southerners.

When Tyler became president, he quickly came into conflict with his own party. He opposed many of their policies, and he vetoed the bills he disagreed with. To get back at him, the Whigs expelled Tyler from their party—leaving him as president with no political party. They nicknamed him "His Accidency." While nine of Tyler's ten vetoes successfully blocked legislation, Congress overrode one on March 3, 1845. It was a minor bill concerned with business contracts for building naval ships. But it was the very first veto in American history to be overridden—more than fifty years after Washington exercised the first veto.

Towers in New York City and the Pentagon in Arlington, Virginia. Nearly three thousand people died in the attack. Republican president George W. Bush responded with military force. First, he launched the War in Afghanistan with the support of Congress and many allied countries. The man who planned the September 11 terror attack, Osama bin Laden, was in Afghanistan at the time. Next, Bush led the American invasion of Iraq. This was far more controversial.

Many countries answered President Bush's call to action in Afghanistan. They sent soldiers and material support to overthrow the government that was hiding Osama bin Laden and set up a new government. There was little question that bin Laden was responsible for September 11. However, the leader

The Twin Towers burn before their collapse on September 11, 2001.

Iraqi dictator Saddam Hussein was captured and executed after the American invasion of Iraq.

of Iraq, Saddam Hussein, had no proven ties to September 11. Bush also said that Hussein had weapons of mass destruction. This includes biological weapons, such as lethal diseases, and chemical weapons, gases that kill and injure. These claims were later found to be false. Additionally, many experts in the American intelligence community had warned Bush that the claims were likely false at the time.

Few allies joined the American invasion of Iraq: one country that did help was Great Britain. Other countries thought Bush's claims about the country were doubtful. The United Nations was inspecting Iraq for weapons of mass destruction at the time and reported that none could be found. However, Bush did receive bipartisan support for the war from Congress.

After the invasion, no weapons program was found. Furthermore, American soldiers started to be killed and wounded more and more. While the Iraqi Army was quickly defeated, an insurgency began. People who opposed the presence of American soldiers in the country took up arms. A civil war between opposing Iraqi factions started. Americans were caught in the middle. By 2007, 3,350 American soldiers had lost their lives in the violence.

A CNN poll in March of 2007 showed that 58 percent of Americans wanted US troops out of Iraq before the end of the year. Both chambers of Congress were narrowly controlled by Democrats, who opposed Republican Bush's handling of the invasion. They passed a bill tying continued military funding of the war to a complete combat troop withdrawal over the next year. Bush vetoed the bill. He argued that an official timeline for withdrawal was "a prescription for chaos and confusion and we must not impose it on our troops."

Democrats were placed in a bad position. They could refuse to fund the military, abandoning them with old equipment in Iraq. That action would obviously be deeply unpopular. So long as combat troops were in Iraq, most people wanted them to be supported. They could not force Bush to withdraw the soldiers because they did not have the votes to override his veto. The House override vote failed to get near the necessary two-thirds. It was just 222 to 203.

As a result, Congress soon passed a bill funding the War in Iraq. Many Democrats voted against the measure, but Republicans were able to secure enough support to pass it. Bush's veto had blocked Congress's demand for a troop withdrawal. However, Democrats in Congress had forced Bush to issue the veto. This tied Bush and Republican lawmakers more tightly to the deeply unpopular war.

Demonstrations against the Iraq War, like this one in Los Angeles, were frequent by 2007.

The Justice Against Sponsors of Terrorism Act

Soon after the September 11 terror attacks, Osama bin Laden became the prime suspect. His responsibility has since been confirmed by the United States government. However, some people have also blamed the government of Saudi Arabia. Fifteen of the nineteen hijackers were from Saudi Arabia. Allegedly, Saudi Arabia also turned a blind eye to some of its citizens who helped fund bin Laden.

Thus far, these allegations remain largely unproven. There is no clear proof that the Saudi government was involved. However, many documents related to the issue remain classified. The relatives of September 11 victims have pushed for the ability to sue the Saudi government for wrongdoing. The suing of a foreign government is a rare occurrence. Typically, governments do not recognize the right of foreign citizens to sue them.

In 2016, Congress passed the Justice Against Sponsors of Terrorism Act (JASTA). It allowed victims of terror attacks and their families to sue foreign governments. The legislation was supported by many family members of victims of September 11. However, President Obama vetoed the bill. He pointed to three reasons for this. First, it would undermine terrorism investigations by moving them to civil court instead of criminal court. Second, it would support the idea that governments could be sued by foreign citizens. If this were applied to the United States, it could result in many lawsuits against the American government. Third, it might stop foreign governments from cooperating in antiterrorism operations. In fact, Saudi Arabia is one of the United States' closest allies in the fight against terrorism. Lawsuits might harm this relationship.

Congress overrode Obama's veto of the bill—the only time in his two terms that a veto was overridden. The bill was hugely popular among both Democrats and

Saudi Arabia is one of the most influential nations in the Middle East.

Republicans. In the Senate, the vote was 97 to 1. In the House, it was 348 to 77.

As of early 2018, a number of lawsuits against Saudi Arabia are working their way through American courts. It is unclear what the result will be. Lawyers representing Saudi Arabia have asked that they be dismissed due to lack of evidence.

A Timeline of Vetoes

June 21, 1788 The Constitution is adopted by the United States. The presidential veto is a key part of its system of checks and balances.

April 5, 1792 George Washington issues the first presidential veto in American history.

January 17, 1822 James Monroe issues what is now considered the first signing statement. It clarified how he would interpret a law.

March 3, 1845 For the first time, Congress overrides a presidential veto, defying President John Tyler.

December 9, 1972 Richard Nixon vetoes the Comprehensive Child Development bill that would have provided childcare for all American children.

April 9, 1996 The Line Item Veto Act is signed into law. It gives the president the power the veto specific lines of budget bills.

June 25, 1998 The Supreme Court rules that the line-item veto is unconstitutional.

May 2, 2007 George W. Bush vetoes a bill requiring American soldiers to be withdrawn from Iraq.

September 23, 2016 Barack Obama vetoes a bill to allow families of terror attack victims to sue foreign governments. His veto is overridden.

IN GOD WE TRUST

4 *What Happens Next?*

After the president vetoes a bill, it is up to Congress how to respond. Sometimes, Congress does not even have a vote to override the veto. It is clear that the president has the support of more than one-third of Congress. Other times, Congress votes and fails to override the veto. Only rarely does Congress successfully override a veto.

Overriding a Veto

Overriding a presidential veto requires a two-thirds majority vote in both the Senate and the House. Typically, this means the president's own party must oppose the

Opposite: Congress has the power to override a presidential veto.

veto. Otherwise, it is a difficult to get this many votes. It is very rare for the party opposed to the president to have a two-thirds majority in both chambers.

Of the 2,574 vetoes between the first veto and the end of Barack Obama's term in 2017, just 111 were overridden. That means less than 5 percent of presidential or pocket vetoes were overridden. If you do not look at pocket vetoes—which cannot be overridden—Congress overrode about 7 percent of presidential vetoes.

In other words, Congress rarely has the support to challenge a presidential veto. This makes the power to veto a bill a very important part of the system of checks and balances. In a divided Congress, the president's veto is often enough to stop a piece of legislation from moving forward. This threat of a veto in turn shapes legislation. Congress tries to make bills that are acceptable to the president.

For some presidents, Congress was able to routinely challenge their vetoes. For example, Andrew Johnson was sworn into office after Lincoln was assassinated. Johnson soon became locked in a bitter conflict with Congress after vetoing an important bill giving newly freed slaves rights. Congress overrode his veto. Of the twenty-one bills that Johnson eventually vetoed, Congress overrode fifteen—a total of 71 percent. The eight pocket vetoes that Johnson used were unable to be overridden. When presidents lack much support in Congress, the power to veto bills has much less sway.

The Decline of the Veto

Recent presidents have vetoed fewer bills than those who came before them. Barack Obama and George W. Bush both vetoed just twelve bills each. Before them, Bill Clinton and George H. W. Bush vetoed thirty-seven and forty-four bills, respectively. Looking even farther back to the middle of the twentieth century, Franklin D. Roosevelt, Harry Truman, and Dwight D. Eisenhower each vetoed more than one hundred.

There are a number of reasons that the use of the veto has declined in recent years. Neither party had a large majority in both chambers of Congress under

Presidents George W. Bush and Barack Obama vetoed relatively few bills.

The Dream of the Line-Item Veto

Ulysses S. Grant was the first president to ask for the power to line-item veto appropriations bills in the 1870s. Presidents after Grant kept asking for the power until Clinton received it in 1996—two years before it was declared unconstitutional. Even though the Supreme Court ruled the line-item veto unconstitutional, presidents have continued to hope it will make a comeback.

In 2006, George W. Bush proposed that Congress give him a different line-item veto power, one that might hold up to a judgment from the Supreme Court. He wanted the power to strike lines from appropriations bills that would then be voted on again by Congress.

In 2010, Barack Obama pushed for something close to a line-item veto as well. He wanted the power to strike out parts of appropriations bills. Then, he wanted Congress to vote to approve or reject the changes without the chance to amend the bill again. Both Bush's and Obama's requests for new powers were ignored by Congress.

On March 23, 2018, Donald Trump signed a $1.3 trillion spending bill. He had previously threatened to veto the bill, which included massive deficit spending. Nevertheless, after signing it, Trump asked Congress to give him the power to line-item veto spending measures. Whether or not Congress grants the power again—and whether the Supreme Court strikes it down—remains to be seen.

Obama or Bush. This makes it difficult for Congress to pass new laws. As a result, there were relatively few bills passed that the president needed to veto. Most bills that were controversial never made it that far in the legislative process.

Additionally, bills have grown larger in recent decades. It has become normal to bundle many separate issues into the same piece of legislation. This is due in part to the difficulty of passing legislation through a divided Congress. When a bill finally does pass, it often legislates a variety of different issues. This makes a veto less likely. The president may disagree with a small part of the bill, but the only choice is to veto the entire bill. When passing legislation is so difficult to begin with, vetoing a major bill is often not appealing.

Getting Involved

On the one hand, the veto is a power that is quite divorced from ordinary Americans. The president and governors are the only people in the country who have the power to veto a bill. The legislative process itself is also quite foreign to most people. While the president and members of Congress are elected by the people, their actions sometimes seem quite far removed from daily life.

Despite these appearances, ordinary Americans can get involved with the legislative process. Citizens can write letters and call their Congresspeople and even the president. The president is the representative of every American, and the members of Congress represent everyone in their district regardless of who they voted for. Directly contacting these lawmakers is the easiest way to weigh in on the legislative process.

Some people also choose to protest or demonstrate on political issues. They might organize rallies where they chant slogans and hold up signs. When the Justice Against Sponsors of Terrorism Act (JASTA) was being considered, many family members of September 11 victims organized in support of the bill. They called Congresspeople and held demonstrations. They waited outside the White House with signs urging Obama not to veto the bill. After he did veto it, they pressured Congress to override the veto.

The Presidential Veto: An Important Power

The veto is a fundamental power of the president. It is written into the Constitution, and it serves as one of the most important checks and balances. The veto is the one official tool that the president has to shape the legislative process.

The president must either veto an entire bill or allow it to become law. The line-item veto was ruled unconstitutional. Signing statements are one way that presidents have tried to get around this requirement, but they are unlikely to hold up in court when they function as line-item vetoes.

Despite the fact that vetoes can only stop an entire bill from becoming law, vetoes do allow the president to impact legislation. When Congress knows that a veto is possible, it often chooses to make legislation that is less controversial. This increases the chance that the president will not veto it. It also means that if the president chooses to veto it, the decision to veto it is more likely to be unpopular.

Protesters urge President Obama not to veto a bill they support.

Vetoes play an important role in political drama in this way. When Democrats forced a bill that would withdraw troops from Iraq through to George W. Bush, they knew that Bush would likely veto the bill. They also knew that they lacked the votes to override it. However, they wanted Bush to be forced to veto the popular measure. This let them say they were doing something to end the war, and to claim that it was the Republicans under Bush who were being unreasonable. Vetoes can help political parties score points.

Throughout American history, the role of vetoes has changed a great deal. At first, they were primarily used to block legislation that the president thought was unconstitutional. However, the role of vetoes gradually expanded, as presidents used them against legislation they simply disagreed with. Despite these changes, vetoes have always been a key part of the American system of checks and balances. Going forward, they will remain an important tool the president has to shape legislation and encourage compromise among lawmakers.

The Keystone XL Pipeline

One controversy of Barack Obama's presidency was the Keystone XL Pipeline. The proposed pipeline would move oil from Canada through the United States to oil refineries. Proponents say the pipeline would create jobs and help the economy. Opponents say the small number of jobs created would not be worth the environmental costs. Oil spills from pipelines can destroy the environment. Also, the pipeline would be supplied with oil extracted from oil sands. This extraction process pollutes Earth more than usual oil drilling.

The Keystone XL Pipeline soon became a political issue. Republican lawmakers campaigned for it to be built. Meanwhile, many Democrats opposed it for environmental reasons. Transnational pipelines, or pipelines spanning more than one country, require the State Department to review and sign off on them. The review process is supposed to determine if the construction is in the national interest.

After the State Department had been reviewing the process for six years, Republican lawmakers grew impatient. With control of Congress, they passed a bill calling for its immediate construction. However, Obama immediately vetoed the measure. Republicans tried to

The Keystone XL Pipeline was meant to carry oil from Canada all the way to Port Arthur on the Gulf of Mexico.

override the veto, but they lacked the votes. Although they had a majority, they did not have the two-thirds necessary for an override. Obama's veto spelled an end to the project during his presidency, but after Donald Trump became president, the State Department soon approved the project.

Glossary

adjournment The period of time when Congress is not meeting.

appropriations bill A bill that assigns money to the government's many departments and agencies.

bill A law before it is passed.

bipartisan Having the support of both major parties. Today, the two parties are the Democrats and Republicans.

budget The planned spending of the government.

controversial Subject to disagreement.

deficit spending Government spending that is greater than the amount of money the government has.

executive The executive branch is headed by the president. It is responsible for enforcing laws and running government departments and agencies.

federal Relating to the country-wide government out of Washington, DC, rather than individual state governments in each of the fifty states.

insurgency A military revolt.

judicial The judicial branch is made up of the courts and judges. It can rule laws unconstitutional.

legislation A law or set of laws.

legislative The legislative branch is made up of the House and Senate. Together, these are known as Congress. Congress is responsible for passing new laws.

opponent Someone who is against something.

override Congress can override a veto (but not a pocket veto) with a two-thirds vote in both chambers. This makes the bill become a law against the president's wishes.

pocket veto A veto that occurs when Congress is not meeting and the president refuses to sign a bill that is passed. It cannot be overridden. However, the president may only pocket veto a bill when Congress stops meeting soon after passing the bill.

proponent Someone who is for something.

protective return The protective return pocket veto is a mix of the pocket veto and presidential veto. It occurs when the president sends a note to Congress saying a bill was pocket vetoed outside of the usual time pocket vetoes can happen. However, Congress tends to treat these vetoes as though they are not pocket vetoes, against the wishes of the president.

unconstitutional Not following the Constitution. It is grounds for a court to overturn a law. Presidents sometimes justify vetoes by saying the bill was unconstitutional to begin with.

veto The president's power to prevent a bill from becoming a law.

Further Information

Books

Frith, Margaret. *Who Was Franklin Roosevelt?* London, UK: Penguin Young Readers Group, 2010.

Harper, Leslie. *Civics Q and A: What are Checks and Balances?* New York: Rosen Publishing Group, 2012.

Websites

Bank War

https://www.history.com/topics/bank-war

History.com looks at the Bank War between Jackson and Congress, including Jackson's historic veto.

How Laws are Made and How to Research Them

https://www.usa.gov/how-laws-are-made

An official website for the US government describes how bills become laws and includes an infographic on the topic.

9 U.S. Presidents with the Most Vetoes

https://www.britannica.com/list/9-us-presidents-with-the-most-vetoes

Mic Anderson profiles the presidents with the most vetoes for the Encyclopedia Britannica.

Videos

FLVS Civics: Foundations - Checks and Balances

https://www.youtube.com/watch?v=6W8W3p9Ot7M

Florida Virtual School reviews the branches of government as well as their checks and balances.

What Is Veto Power?

https://www.history.com/topics/veto/videos/what-is-veto-power

History.com explains how the veto works and looks at some historical cases.

Bibliography

Bomboy, Scott. "A Brief Look at How Presidents Use Veto Power in Difficult Situations." Constitution Daily, November 10, 2014. https://constitutioncenter.org/blog/a-brief-look-at-how-presidents-use-veto-power-in-difficult-situations.

Cohen, Nancy L. "Why America Never Had Universal Child Care." *New Republic*, April 23, 2013. https://newrepublic.com/article/113009/child-care-america-was-very-close-universal-day-care.

Fisher, Louis. "The Pocket Veto: Its Current Status." *CRS Report for Congress*, March 30, 2001. https://www.senate.gov/reference/resources/pdf/RL30909.pdf.

Flaherty, Anne, and Jennifer Loven. "Bush Vetoes Troop Withdrawal Bill." *Washington Post*, May 2, 2007. http://www.washingtonpost.com/wp-dyn/content/article/2007/05/01/AR2007050101222.html.

Holloway, Carson. *Hamilton versus Jefferson in the Washington Administration: Completing the Founding or Betraying the Founding?* Cambridge, UK: Cambridge University Press, 2015.

Kirby, Jen. "Trump Wants a Line-Item Veto. One Problem: It's Unconstitutional." *Vox*, March 23, 2018. https://www.vox.com/2018/3/23/17157130/trump-omnibus-spending-line-item-veto-clinton.

Mason, Jeff, and Richard Cowan. "Obama Vetoes Keystone XL Pipeline Bill." *Scientific American*, February 24, 2015. https://www.scientificamerican.com/article/obama-vetoes-keystone-xl-pipeline-bill.

Mondale, Walter. *The Good Fight: A Life in Liberal Politics.* New York: Scribner, 2010.

Office of the Historian. "Presidential Vetoes." US House of Representatives, August 16, 2017. http://history.house.gov/Institution/Presidential-Vetoes/Presidential-Vetoes.

Woolley, John T. "Presidential Signing Statements." American Presidency Project. Retrieved May 1, 2018. http://www.presidency.ucsb.edu/signingstatements.php.

Index

Page numbers in **boldface** are illustrations.

About the Author

Derek Miller is a writer and educator from Salisbury, Maryland. He is the author of many books for young readers, including *How Government Works: Collecting Taxes* and *How Government Works: Executive Orders.* When he's not writing or teaching, Miller enjoys traveling with his wife.